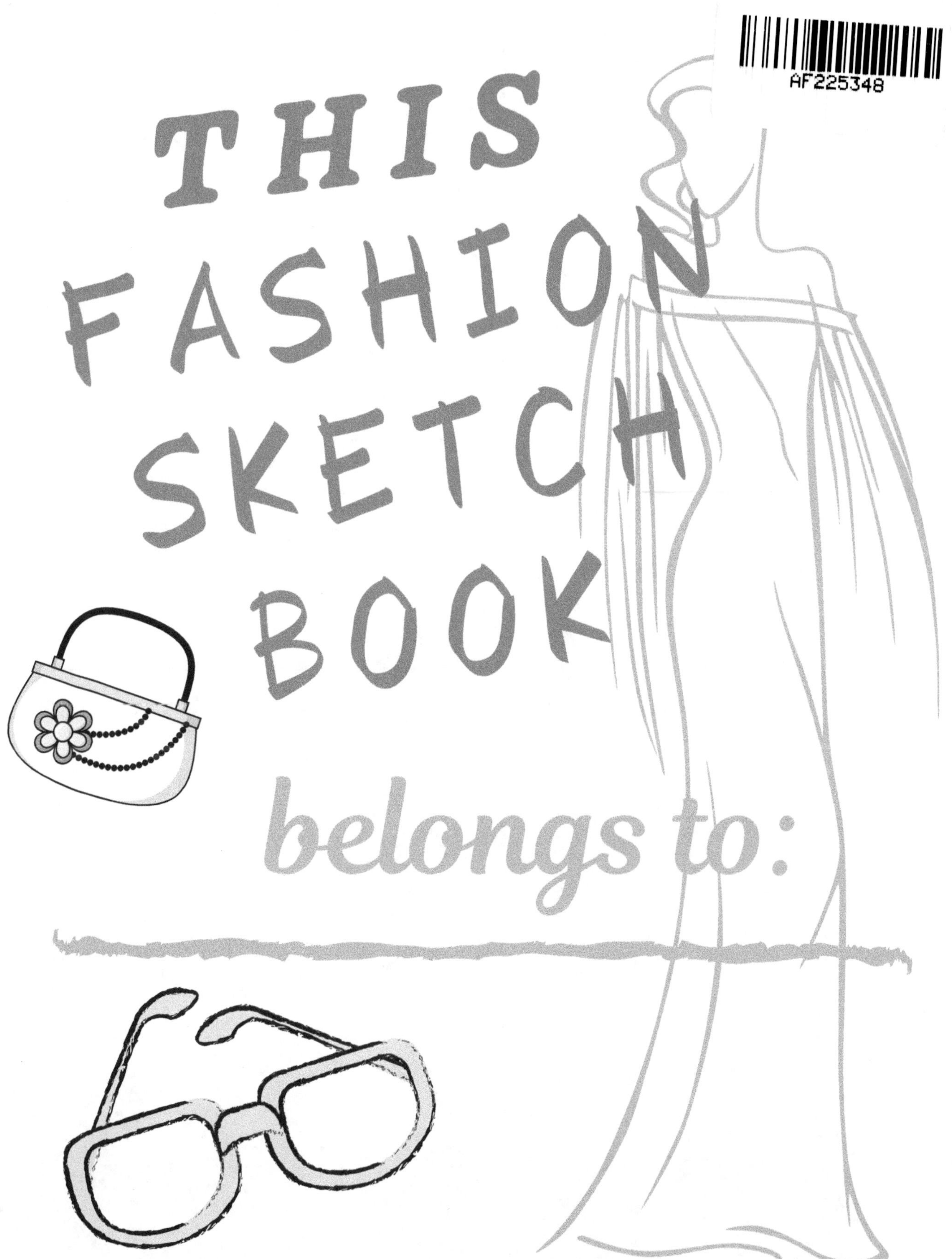

THIS
FASHION
SKETCH
BOOK
belongs to:
AF225348

DEDICATION

This Fashion Sketchbook Journal is dedicated to all the fashionistas out there who love to design clothing and document their findings in the process.

You are my inspiration for producing books and I'm honored to be a part of keeping all of your Fashion Sketch notes, and records organized.

This journal notebook will help you record your details about your beautiful designs.

Thoughtfully put together with these sections to record: Female Templates, Styles, Trends, Inspiration, Textiles, Notes, Details, & Swatches.

HOW TO USE THIS BOOK

The purpose of this book is to keep all of your Fashion Sketchbook notes all in one place. It will help keep you organized.

This Fashion Sketchbook will allow you to accurately document every detail about your designs. It's a great way to chart your course by creating beautiful clothing.

Here are examples of the prompts for you to fill in and write about your experience in this book:

* 1. Female Templates - Use to design your own clothing.

* 2. Styles - Write the style you are going for.

* 3. Trends - Log any trends you want to design.

* 4. Inspiration - Record where your inspiration for this design came from.

* 5. Textiles - Write what the clothing is to be made of.

* 6. Notes - Log any other important information.

* 7. Details - Record any details about the garment.

* 8. Swatches - A place to attach your swatches.

Style ____

Trends ____

____

Inspiration ____

____

Textiles ____

____

Notes ____

____

Swatches

Details

Style _______________________________

Trends _______________________________
____
____

Inspiration _______________________________
____

Textiles _______________________________
____
____

Notes _______________________________
____

Swatches

Details

Style ____

Trends ____

____

Inspiration ____

____

Textiles ____

____

Notes ____

____

Swatches

Details

Style _______________________________

Trends _______________________________

____

Inspiration _______________________________

____

Textiles _______________________________

____

Notes _______________________________

____

Swatches

Details

Style _______________________________

Trends _______________________________
____

Inspiration _______________________________
____

Textiles _______________________________
____

Notes _______________________________
____

Swatches

Details

Style

Trends

Inspiration

Textiles

Notes

Swatches

Details

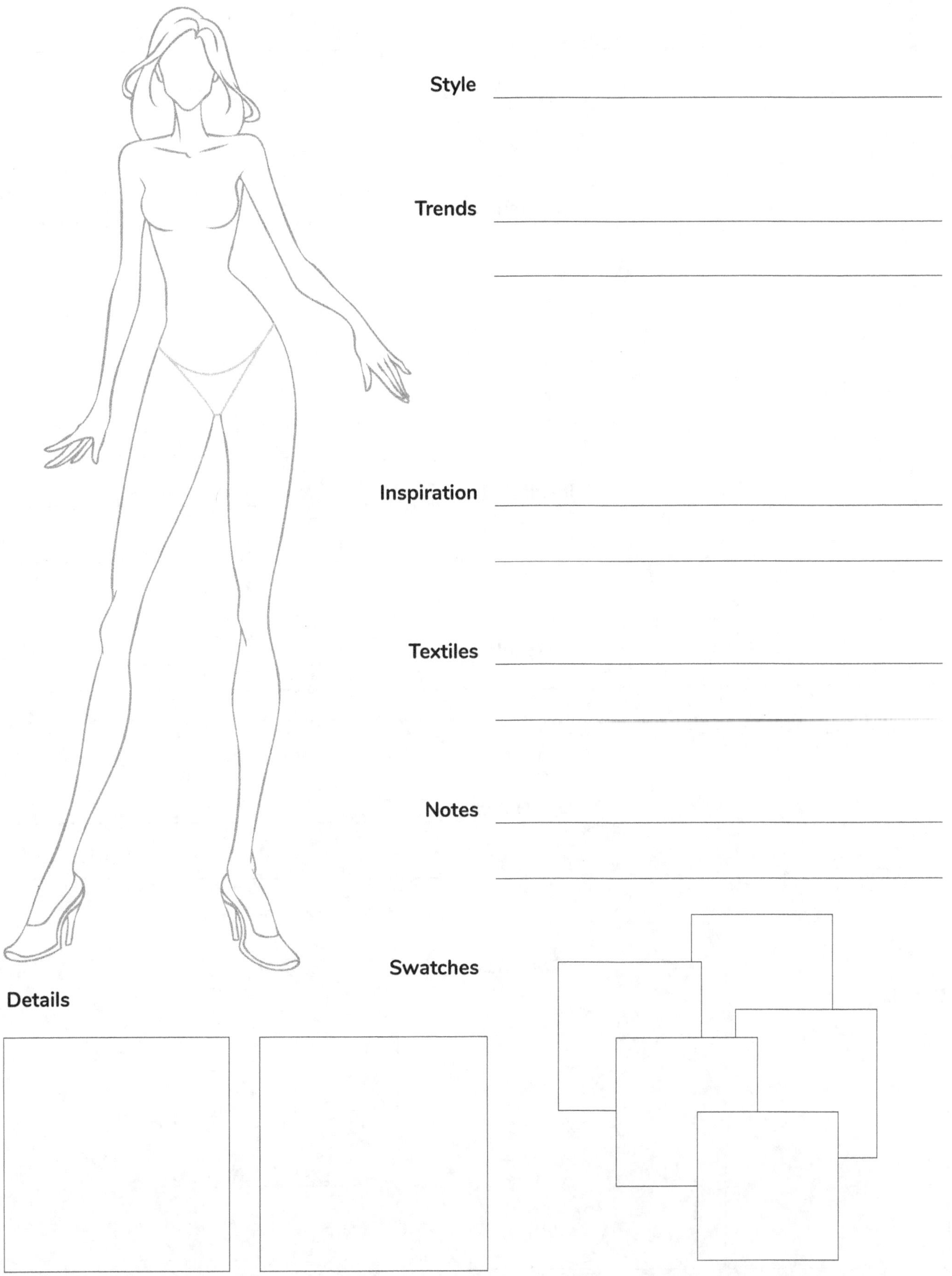

Style

Trends

Inspiration

Textiles

Notes

Swatches

Details

Style ___________________________

Trends ___________________________

Inspiration ___________________________

Textiles ___________________________

Notes ___________________________

Swatches

Details

Style _______________________________

Trends _______________________________

____

Inspiration _______________________________

____

Textiles _______________________________

____

Notes _______________________________

____

Swatches

Details

Style

Trends

Inspiration

Textiles

Notes

Swatches

Details

Style

Trends

Inspiration

Textiles

Notes

Swatches

Details

Style ____

Trends ____

____

Inspiration ____

____

Textiles ____

____

Notes ____

____

Swatches

Details

Style

Trends

Inspiration

Textiles

Notes

Swatches

Details

Style ____________________

Trends ____________________

Inspiration ____________________

Textiles ____________________

Notes ____________________

Swatches

Details

Style

Trends

Inspiration

Textiles

Notes

Swatches

Details

Style

Trends

Inspiration

Textiles

Notes

Swatches

Details

Style ____

Trends ____

____

Inspiration ____

____

Textiles ____

____

Notes ____

____

Swatches

Details

Style

Trends

Inspiration

Textiles

Notes

Swatches

Details

Style ___________________________

Trends ___________________________

____

Inspiration ___________________________

____

Textiles ___________________________

____

Notes ___________________________

____

Swatches

Details

Style

Trends

Inspiration

Textiles

Notes

Swatches

Details

Style _______________________________

Trends _______________________________

____

Inspiration _______________________________

____

Textiles _______________________________

____

Notes _______________________________

____

Swatches

Details

Style

Trends

Inspiration

Textiles

Notes

Swatches

Details

Style

Trends

Inspiration

Textiles

Notes

Swatches

Details

Style

Trends

Inspiration

Textiles

Notes

Swatches

Details

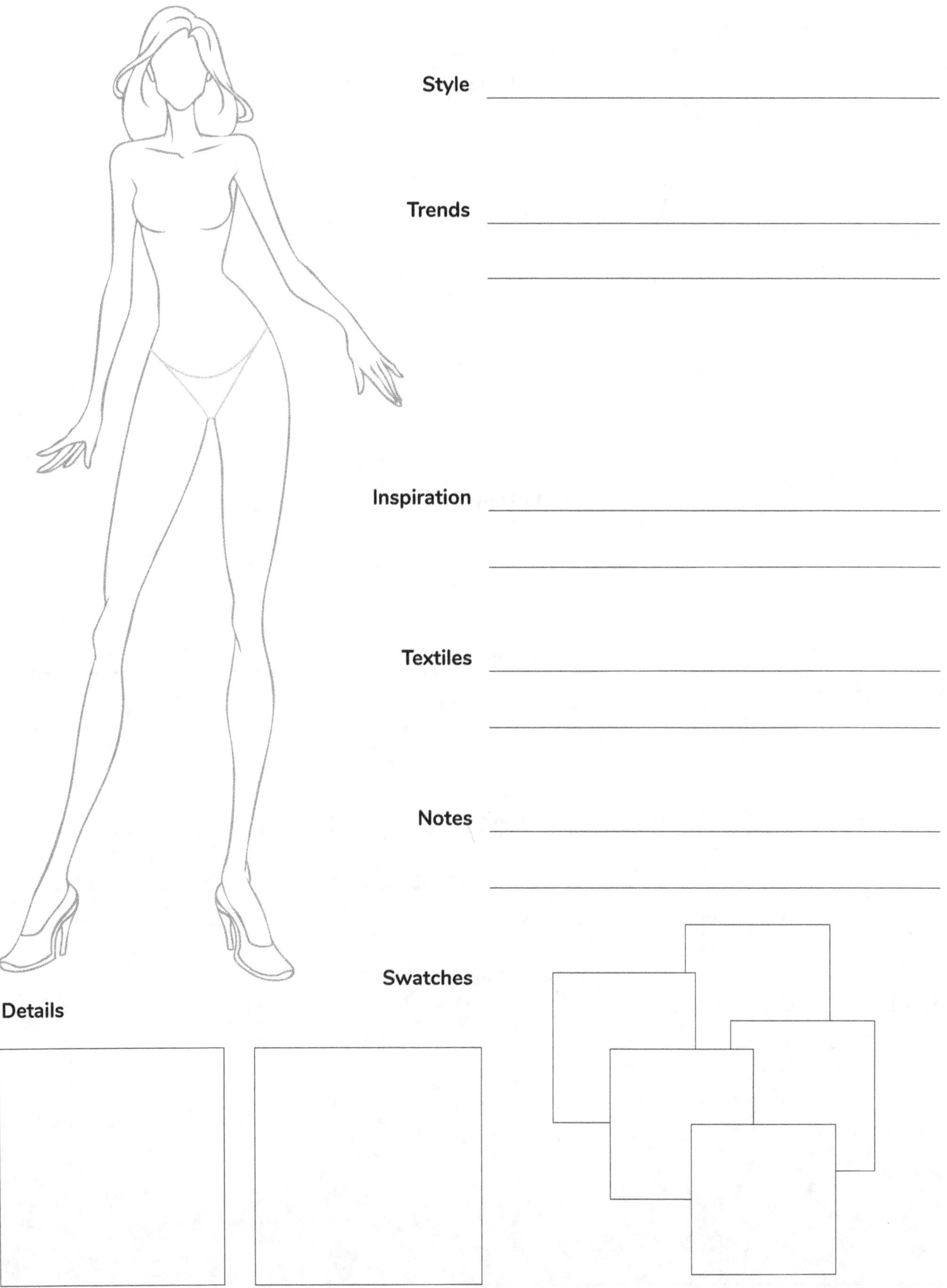

Style

Trends

Inspiration

Textiles

Notes

Swatches

Details

Style

Trends

Inspiration

Textiles

Notes

Swatches

Details

Style ________________________________

Trends ________________________________

____

Inspiration ________________________________

____

Textiles ________________________________

____

Notes ________________________________

____

Details

Swatches

Style _______________________________________

Trends _______________________________________
____

Inspiration _______________________________________
____

Textiles _______________________________________
____

Notes _______________________________________
____

Swatches

Details

Style

Trends

Inspiration

Textiles

Notes

Swatches

Details

Style ___________________________

Trends ___________________________
____
____

Inspiration ___________________________
____

Textiles ___________________________
____

Notes ___________________________
____

Swatches

Details

Style _______________________________

Trends _______________________________
____
____

Inspiration _______________________________
____

Textiles _______________________________
____

Notes _______________________________
____

Swatches

Details

Style _______________________________

Trends _______________________________

____

Inspiration _______________________________

____

Textiles _______________________________

____

Notes _______________________________

____

Swatches

Details

Style

Trends

Inspiration

Textiles

Notes

Swatches

Details

Style _______________________

Trends _______________________

____

Inspiration _______________________

____

Textiles _______________________

____

Notes _______________________

____

Swatches

Details

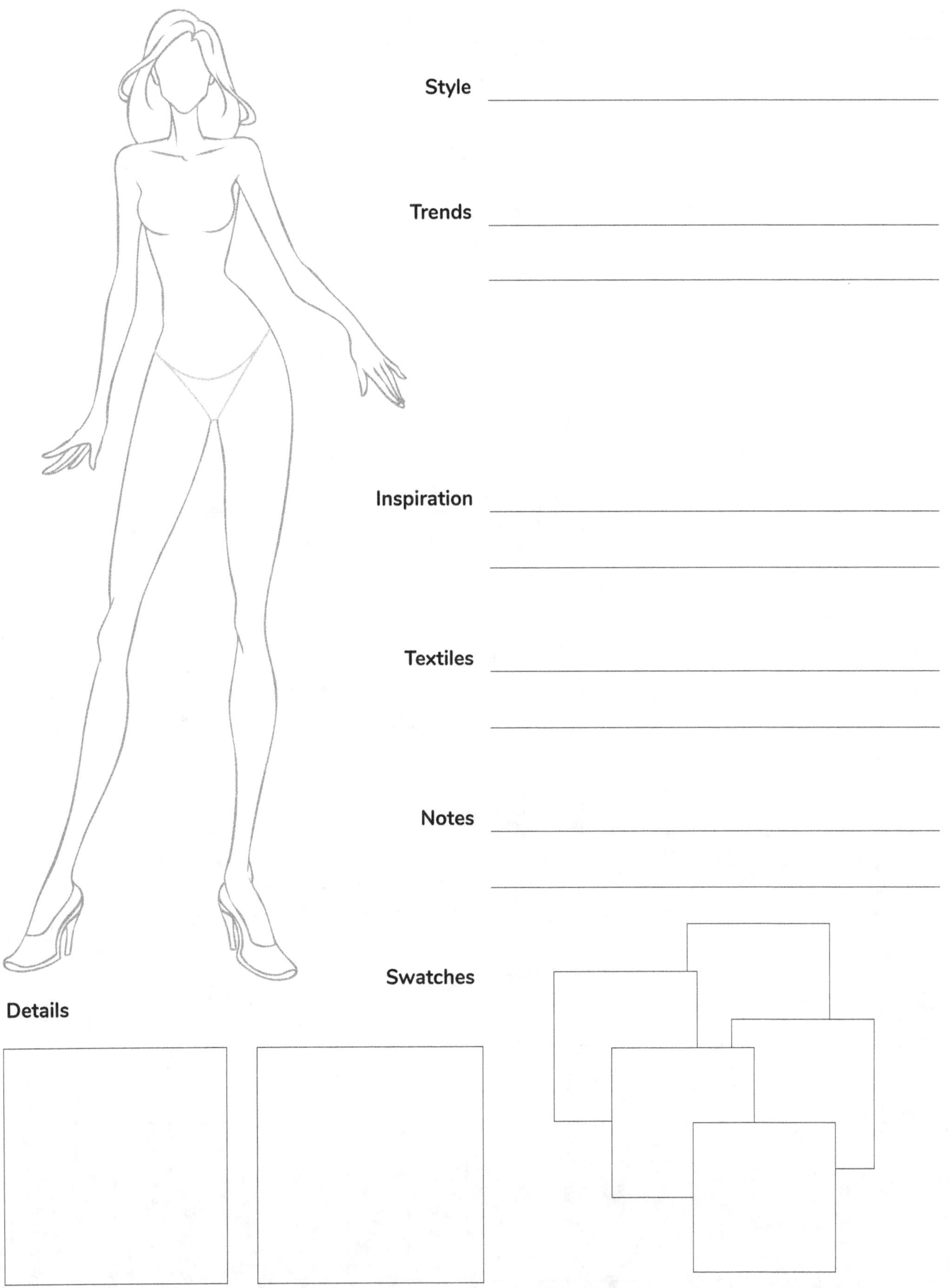

Style

Trends

Inspiration

Textiles

Notes

Swatches

Details

Style

Trends

Inspiration

Textiles

Notes

Swatches

Details

Style _______________________________

Trends _______________________________

____

Inspiration _______________________________

____

Textiles _______________________________

____

Notes _______________________________

____

Swatches

Details

Style

Trends

Inspiration

Textiles

Notes

Swatches

Details

Style ___________________________

Trends ___________________________

____

Inspiration ___________________________

____

Textiles ___________________________

____

Notes ___________________________

____

Swatches

Details

Style ______________________________

Trends ______________________________

Inspiration ______________________________

Textiles ______________________________

Notes ______________________________

Swatches

Details

Style ___________________________

Trends ___________________________

____

Inspiration ___________________________

____

Textiles ___________________________

____

Notes ___________________________

____

Swatches

Details

Style ______________________________

Trends ______________________________

Inspiration ______________________________

Textiles ______________________________

Notes ______________________________

Swatches

Details

Style ______________________________

Trends ______________________________

____

Inspiration ______________________________

____

Textiles ______________________________

____

Notes ______________________________

____

Details

Swatches

Style

Trends

Inspiration

Textiles

Notes

Swatches

Details

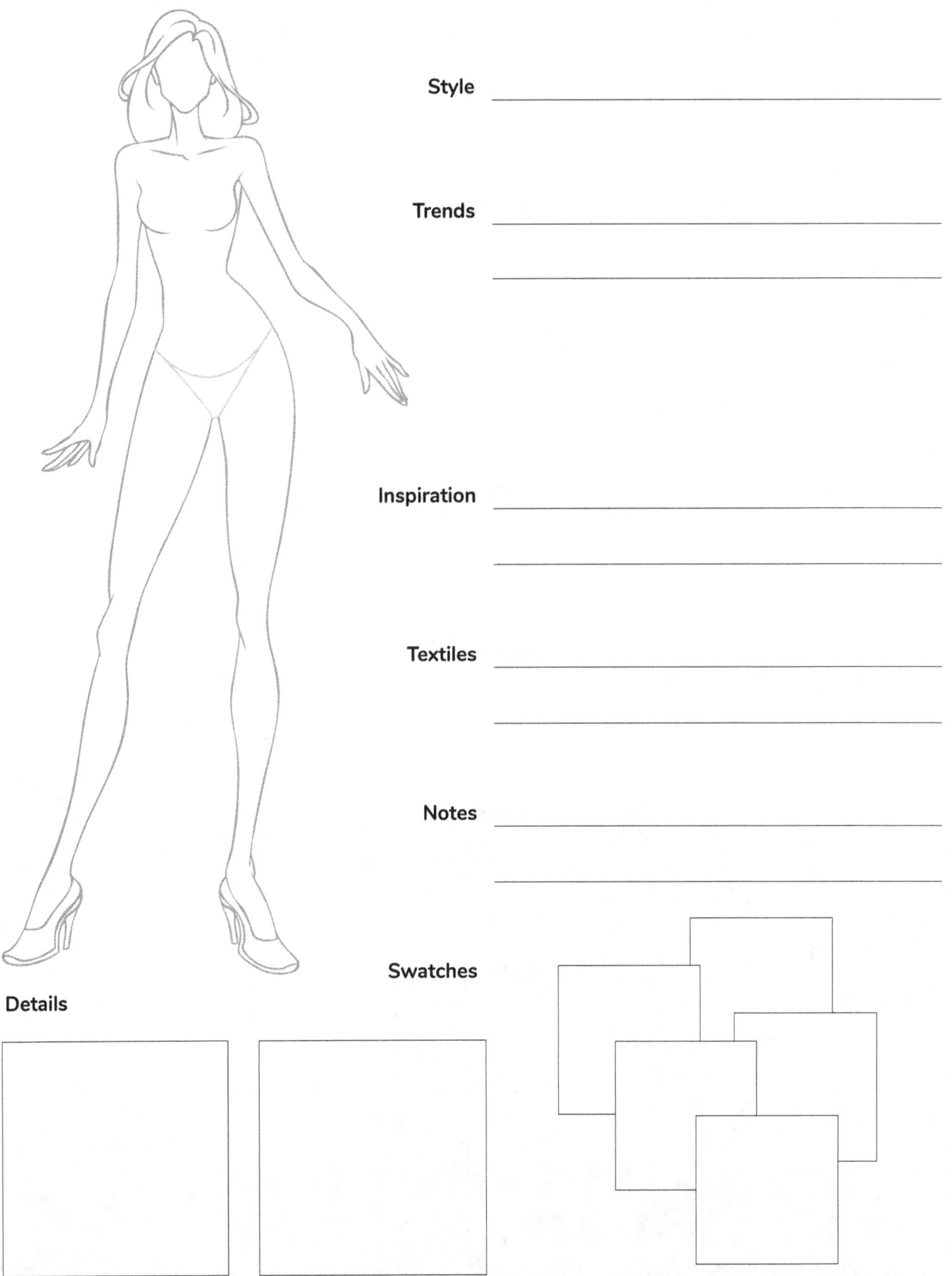

Style

Trends

Inspiration

Textiles

Notes

Swatches

Details

Style

Trends

Inspiration

Textiles

Notes

Swatches

Details

Style ________________________________

Trends ________________________________

____

Inspiration ________________________________

____

Textiles ________________________________

____

Notes ________________________________

____

Swatches

Details

Style

Trends

Inspiration

Textiles

Notes

Swatches

Details

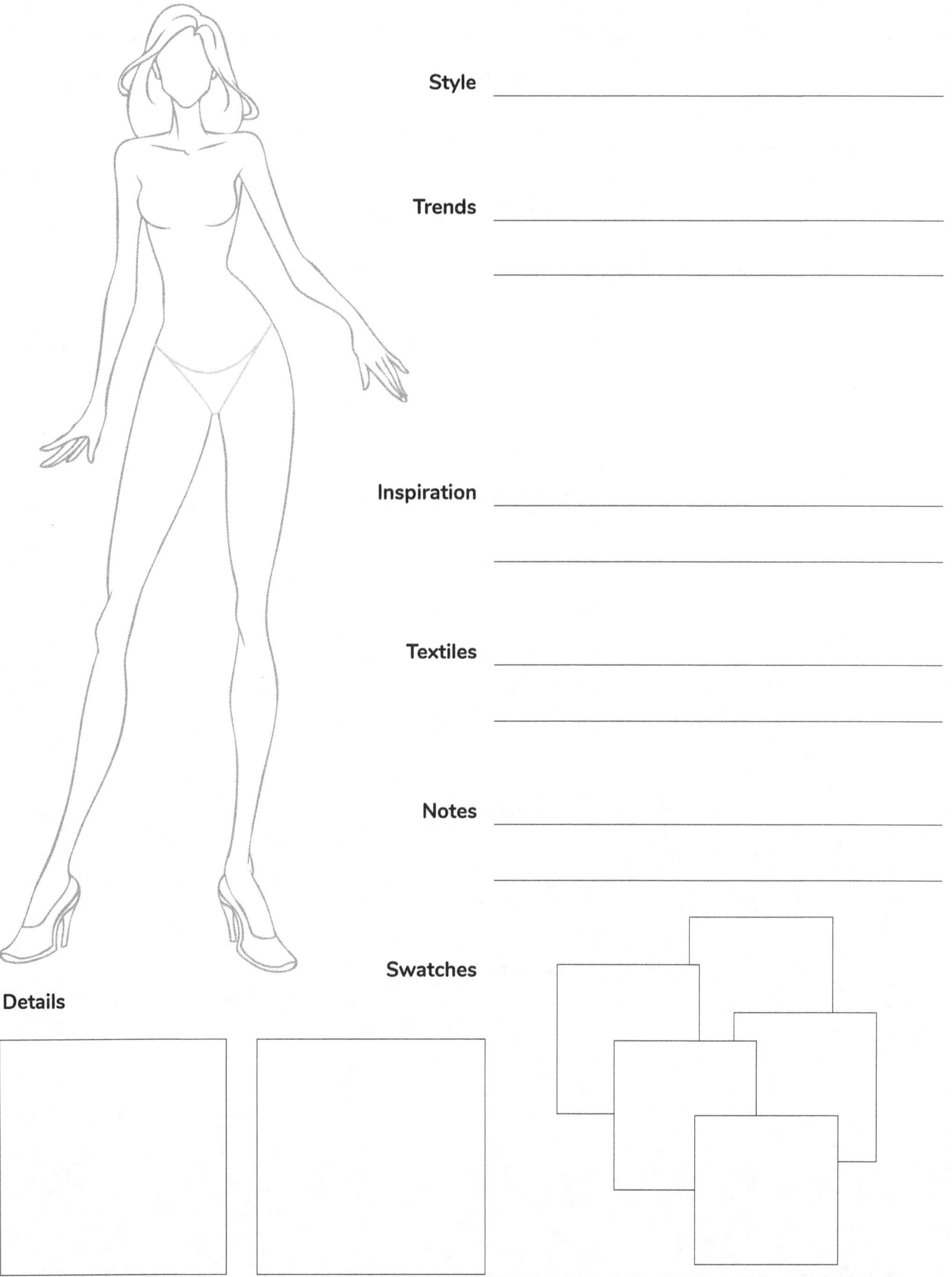

Style
Trends
Inspiration
Textiles
Notes
Swatches
Details

Style ______________________________

Trends ______________________________

Inspiration ______________________________

Textiles ______________________________

Notes ______________________________

Swatches

Details

Style ___________________________

Trends ___________________________
____

Inspiration ___________________________
____

Textiles ___________________________
____

Notes ___________________________
____

Swatches

Details

Style

Trends

Inspiration

Textiles

Notes

Swatches

Details

Style ______________________________

Trends ______________________________
____

Inspiration ______________________________
____

Textiles ______________________________
____

Notes ______________________________
____

Swatches

Details

Style

Trends

Inspiration

Textiles

Notes

Swatches

Details

Style ____

Trends ____

____

Inspiration ____

____

Textiles ____

____

Notes ____

____

Swatches

Details

Style

Trends

Inspiration

Textiles

Notes

Swatches

Details

Style

Trends

Inspiration

Textiles

Notes

Swatches

Details

Style _______________________________

Trends _______________________________
____
____

Inspiration _______________________________
____

Textiles _______________________________
____
____

Notes _______________________________
____

Swatches

Details

Style _______________________

Trends _______________________
____

Inspiration _______________________
____

Textiles _______________________
____

Notes _______________________
____

Swatches

Details

Style ___________________________________

Trends ___________________________________
____
____

Inspiration ___________________________________
____

Textiles ___________________________________
____

Notes ___________________________________
____

Swatches

Details

Style _______________________________

Trends _______________________________

____

Inspiration _______________________________

____

Textiles _______________________________

____

Notes _______________________________

____

Swatches

Details

Style

Trends

Inspiration

Textiles

Notes

Swatches

Details

Style ___________________________

Trends ___________________________
____

Inspiration ___________________________
____

Textiles ___________________________
____

Notes ___________________________
____

Swatches

Details

Style

Trends

Inspiration

Textiles

Notes

Swatches

Details

Style _______________________________________

Trends _______________________________________

____

Inspiration _______________________________________

____

Textiles _______________________________________

____

Notes _______________________________________

____

Swatches

Details

Style

Trends

Inspiration

Textiles

Notes

Swatches

Details

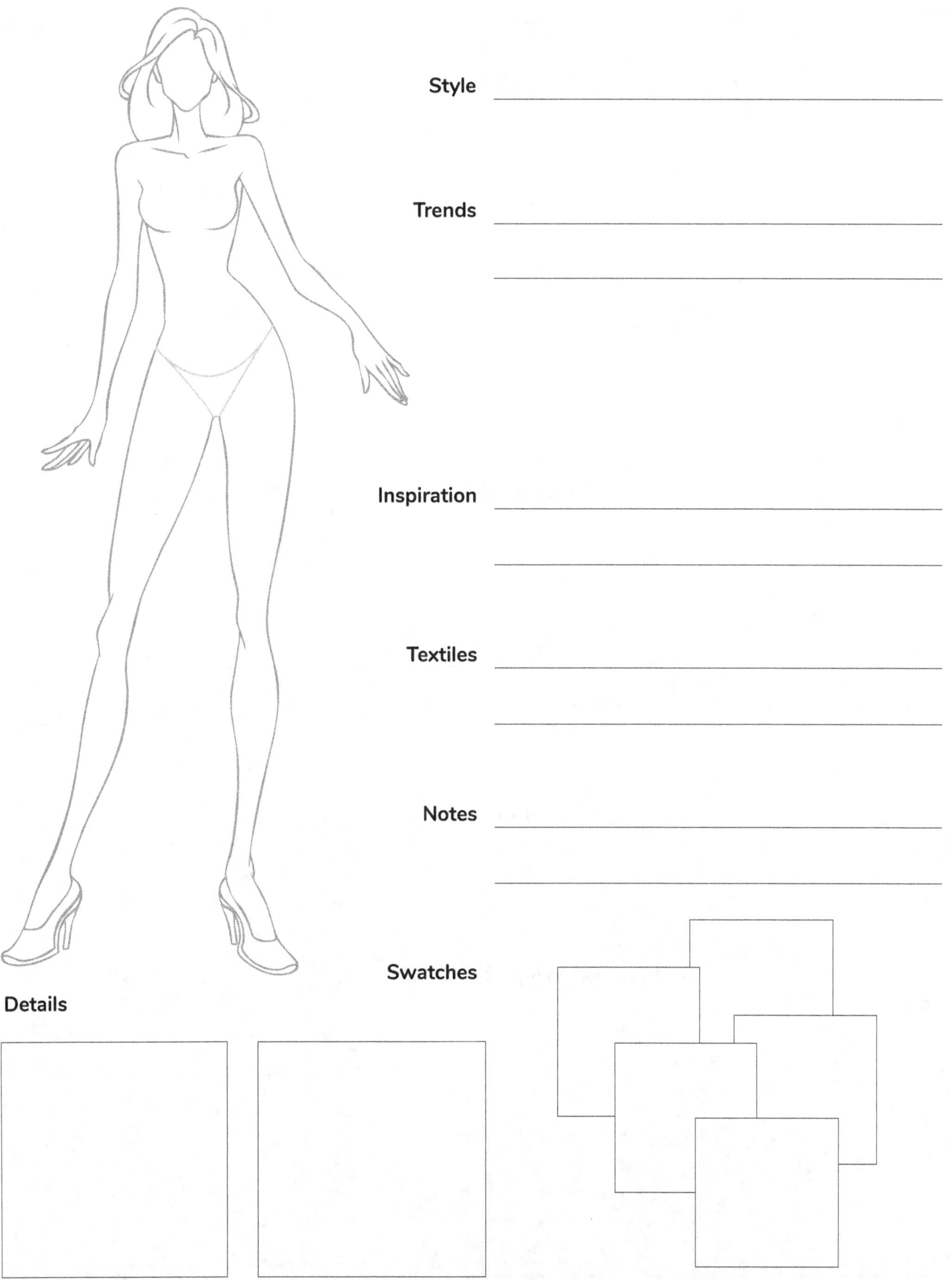

Style
Trends
Inspiration
Textiles
Notes
Swatches
Details

Style

Trends

Inspiration

Textiles

Notes

Details

Swatches

Style ______________________________

Trends ______________________________

Inspiration ______________________________

Textiles ______________________________

Notes ______________________________

Swatches

Details

Style ___________________________

Trends ___________________________
____

Inspiration ___________________________
____

Textiles ___________________________
____

Notes ___________________________
____

Swatches

Details

Style ___________________________________

Trends ___________________________________

____

Inspiration ___________________________________

____

Textiles ___________________________________

____

Notes ___________________________________

____

Swatches

Details

Style ___________________________

Trends ___________________________

____

Inspiration ___________________________

____

Textiles ___________________________

____

Notes ___________________________

____

Swatches

Details

Style

Trends

Inspiration

Textiles

Notes

Swatches

Details

Style ______________________________

Trends ______________________________

Inspiration ______________________________

Textiles ______________________________

Notes ______________________________

Swatches

Details

Style _______________________________________

Trends _______________________________________
____
____

Inspiration _______________________________________
____

Textiles _______________________________________
____
____

Notes _______________________________________
____

Swatches

Details

Style

Trends

Inspiration

Textiles

Notes

Swatches

Details

Style ___________________________

Trends ___________________________

____

Inspiration ___________________________

____

Textiles ___________________________

____

Notes ___________________________

____

Swatches

Details

Style _______________________________

Trends _______________________________

____

Inspiration _______________________________

____

Textiles _______________________________

____

Notes _______________________________

____

Swatches

Details

Style ___________________________

Trends ___________________________

____

Inspiration ___________________________

____

Textiles ___________________________

____

Notes ___________________________

____

Swatches

Details

Style ____

Trends ____

____

Inspiration ____

____

Textiles ____

____

Notes ____

____

Swatches

Details

Style _______________________________

Trends _______________________________

____

Inspiration _______________________________

____

Textiles _______________________________

____

Notes _______________________________

____

Swatches

Details

Style ____

Trends ____
____
____

Inspiration ____

____

Textiles ____

____

Notes ____

____

Swatches

Details

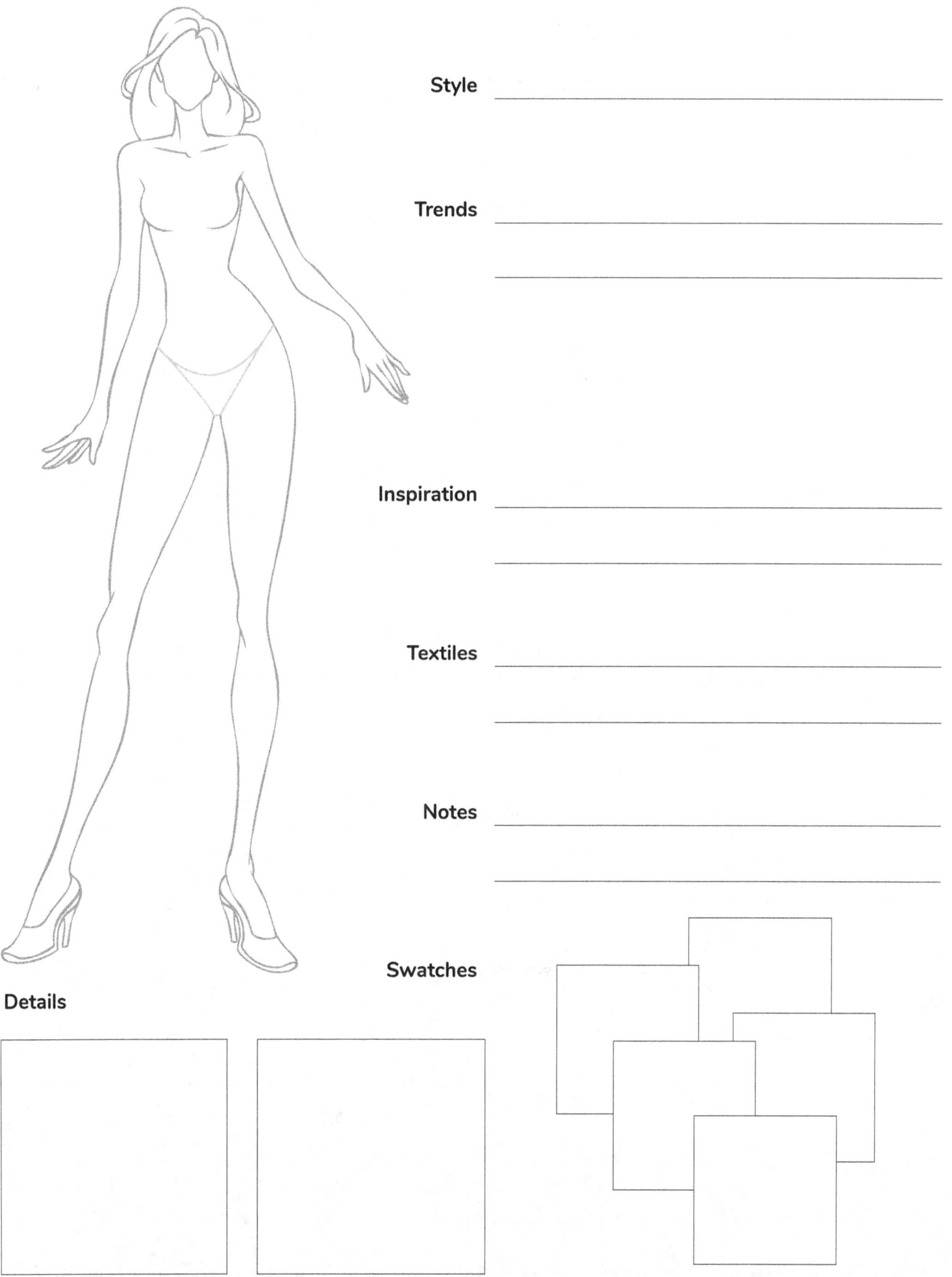

Style
Trends
Inspiration
Textiles
Notes
Swatches
Details

Style

Trends

Inspiration

Textiles

Notes

Swatches

Details

Style ______________________________

Trends ______________________________

____

Inspiration ______________________________

____

Textiles ______________________________

____

Notes ______________________________

____

Swatches

Details

Style _______________________________

Trends _______________________________

____

Inspiration _______________________________

____

Textiles _______________________________

____

Notes _______________________________

____

Swatches

Details

Style

Trends

Inspiration

Textiles

Notes

Swatches

Details

Style

Trends

Inspiration

Textiles

Notes

Swatches

Details

Style _______________________________________

Trends _______________________________________

____

Inspiration _______________________________________

____

Textiles _______________________________________

____

Notes _______________________________________

____

Swatches

Details

Style _______________________________

Trends _______________________________
____
____

Inspiration _______________________________

____

Textiles _______________________________

____

Notes _______________________________

____

Swatches

Details

Style ____

Trends ____

____

____

Inspiration ______________________________________

____

Textiles ____

____

Notes ____

____

Swatches

Details

Style

Trends

Inspiration

Textiles

Notes

Swatches

Details

Style ____

Trends ____
____

Inspiration ____
____

Textiles ____
____

Notes ____
____

Swatches

Details

Style ____________________________

Trends ____________________________
____
____

Inspiration ____________________________
____

Textiles ____________________________
____

Notes ____________________________
____

Swatches

Details

Style

Trends

Inspiration

Textiles

Notes

Swatches

Details

Style

Trends

Inspiration

Textiles

Notes

Swatches

Details

Style ____

Trends ____

____

Inspiration ____

____

Textiles ____

____

Notes ____

____

Swatches

Details

Style _______________________

Trends _______________________

Inspiration _______________________

Textiles _______________________

Notes _______________________

Swatches

Details

Style _______________________________

Trends _______________________________

____

Inspiration _______________________________

____

Textiles _______________________________

____

Notes _______________________________

____

Details

Swatches

Style _______________________________

Trends _______________________________
____

Inspiration _______________________________
____

Textiles _______________________________
____

Notes _______________________________
____

Swatches

Details

Style ______________________________

Trends ______________________________
____

Inspiration ______________________________
____

Textiles ______________________________
____

Notes ______________________________
____

Swatches

Details

Style

____

Trends

____

____

Inspiration

____

____

Textiles

____

____

Notes

____

____

Swatches

Details

Style

Trends

Inspiration

Textiles

Notes

Swatches

Details

Style

Trends

Inspiration

Textiles

Notes

Swatches

Details

Style _______________________________

Trends _______________________________
____

Inspiration _______________________________
____

Textiles _______________________________
____

Notes _______________________________
____

Swatches

Details

Style

Trends

Inspiration

Textiles

Notes

Swatches

Details

Style

Trends

Inspiration

Textiles

Notes

Swatches

Details

Style ______________________________

Trends ______________________________

____

Inspiration ______________________________

____

Textiles ______________________________

____

Notes ______________________________

____

Swatches

Details